PERFECTLY LOVED

Discovering the Blessings Raising a Child with Special Needs

Ana Munoz

First published by Ultimate World Publishing 2023
Copyright © 2023 Ana Munoz

ISBN

Paperback: 978-1-922982-62-9
Ebook: 978-1-922982-63-6

Ana Munoz has asserted her rights under the Copyright, Designs and Patents Act 1988 to be identified as the author of this work. The information in this book is based on the author's experiences and opinions. The publisher specifically disclaims responsibility for any adverse consequences which may result from use of the information contained herein. Permission to use information has been sought by the author. Any breaches will be rectified in further editions of the book.

All rights reserved. No part of this publication may be reproduced, stored in or introduced into a retrieval system, or transmitted in any form, or by any means (electronic, mechanical, photocopying, recording or otherwise) without the prior written permission of the author. Any person who does any unauthorized act in relation to this publication may be liable to criminal prosecution and civil claims for damages. Enquiries should be made through the publisher.

Cover design: Ultimate World Publishing
Layout and typesetting: Ultimate World Publishing
Editor: Vanessa McKay

Ultimate World Publishing
Diamond Creek,
Victoria Australia 3089
www.writeabook.com.au

Testimonials

I met Ana in 2010. I sat across from her in a camp dining hall full of kids as she shared her passion for her beautiful special needs daughter. And then she shared her vision for special needs kids in the Hawaiian Islands. In those few minutes I was captured by her passion, vision and love for her daughter.
Ana cares for all special needs kids, not just her own.

She is fearless, determined, full of faith and love for Jesus.
She greatly impacted my life, but I am only one of many. I count myself blessed to call her friend.

Nick Palermo
Founder of Young Life Capernaum, Executive Founding Director
Emmaus Inn Ministries

I have known Ana Munoz since 2005 and have continuously witnessed her enormous love for not only her own special needs child, but with unbridled enthusiasm, Ana shares that same love with every challenged child she comes in contact with.

With our Camp Agape Teams we have been able to assist Ana with her special needs proms and some Special Camp events which overjoyed the children and encouraged us all.

The world is blessed by Ana's creativity, strength and commitment in loving on God's special children.

Rudy Bosma
Camp Agape Kauai
Former Director

I met Ana in 2008 when she lovingly welcomed my family into hers after moving to Kauai. Since the day I met her, I knew she had a deep love and desire to encourage and inspire individuals with special needs. Her passion led her to start Young Life Capernaum, the only outreach on Kauai for young people with intellectual and physical disabilities. Ana's vision was to create a place where young people with special needs could come and know God's love for them all while having fun. Ana's vision expanded to monthly clubs, weekly Bible studies, sign language performances, proms and summer camps for these special young people.

Our Island and our hearts have forever been impacted by Ana's love, leadership and passion for individuals with special needs to be all that God created them to be. She has a special gift to make people feel loved and she serves others with unrelenting joy. I have personally seen her lovingly parent her daughter throughout the years and encourage her that the sky is the limit. Ana leaves a bright light in all of the hearts of the people she meets. You will forever be challenged, encouraged and blessed by Ana's wisdom and passion for individuals with special needs. Our community has been transformed by her love.

Thanks,
Amanda Phillips
Occupational Therapist Able Ministries

Ana is a woman I would describe as courageous. She is authentic in honesty, brave in embracing life 's difficulties, and extremely devoted.

She is full of zest for life! This is why she has been such an effectual force in uplifting and empowering many in our special-needs community here on Kaua'i.

Angela Rice
Preschool Teacher for 25 years

Ana lives out her love and passion with enthusiasm for the special needs community. She embraces their differences and believes that 'they can' which spills over into their lives. She is an advocate and champion for them and helps them to believe in themselves. I am so blessed to know Ana and the great impact that she has had on my daughter, Sarah's life.

Sharon Peck
Parent, Nurse, Teacher and Coach
For Special Needs Community

I met Ana in 2011 at our local church. She was a tireless leader for special needs kids. She had boundless energy and infectious enthusiasm that spilled over to the volunteers and participants. I remember being impressed by her dedication not only to her daughter, but to all the children.

A few years later, Ana and I connected professionally. She continues to be an advocate for her daughter and the people she works with. She does this work not because she must, but because of her giving heart. Ana seems to find time to support several clients, organize monthly craft activities, take care of her mother, lead Bible studies, and support the developmentally disabled community on Kauai. Ana has a strong faith that resonates and knows no boundaries. I am blessed to know Ana as a colleague, a friend, and a prayer warrior.

Julie Anderson
Division Director
BAYADA Habilitation

As a mum of a young man who lives with Down syndrome, I have thoroughly enjoyed reading about their story and related to many things Ana shared in her book.

Ana's book is a wonderful read sharing her experiences with honesty and this book will be a great resource for so many to read.

The directions we thought we were heading may have changed when our children joined our families, but the journey we are on is amazing. Congratulations Ana, on a wonderful book that so many will enjoy and learn about things they may not ever have had a chance to learn about without your book.

Julie Fisher
Author, *The Unexpected Journey: Embracing the Beauty of Disability*, *The Magic Of Inclusion: Give People A Chance And Watch Them Shine* **and** *From the Hearts of Mums, Stories of Love and Inclusion in the World of Down Syndrome*

Disclaimer

Expressions of innocence or guilt are my opinion. These expressions are backed by actual events. This is a work of nonfiction. Some names and characters have been changed. I have deliberately obscured some identifying features of characters in this book both for legal and moral reasons and in some instances, dates, locations and other identifiers have been changed to protect those that need protecting.

I do not presume to tell the story of others who feature predominantly in this book. Their feelings, emotions, thoughts and memories are their own and they deserve the respect I give them by only writing about them what is necessary in telling my own story. This is my perspective only.

Neither the author nor the publisher will be held liable or responsible for any actual or perceived loss or damage to any person or entity, caused or alleged to have been caused, directly or indirectly, by what's written in this book.

This book may trigger painful memories. Please seek help from someone if this occurs. Please see the back of this book for contact details and help available.

Acknowledgements

To **God** Be the Glory, He continues to do remarkable things in my life.

To **Pedro Adao, The 100x Team, Holli Peel, and Kingdom Seekers**. You taught me how to wake up to my dream and take action.

I hereby acknowledge with gratitude to the **Ultimate World Publishing Team** who taught me that there is an author in me and helped me through every step to get there.

I would like to acknowledge my Graphic Designer **Nikola Boskovski**. I am so pleased with the Design.

To my **dear friends** who supported me and prayed for me daily, through my new journey.

To the **Garden Island Newspaper,** who authored many articles about my daughter, the special needs organizations and family business, I have been involved in for many years.
Mahalo!

You can Connect with Ana Munoz and see what's coming up next.

P o Box 153
Hanamaulu, Hi 96715
Website: https://perfectlylovely@anamunozlive.com
Email: perfectlylovely8400@gmail.com
Instagram: Anamunoz8400

Dedicated to...

My perfectly made daughter, who has taught me more than she will ever know. To my Heavenly Father, who helped me be strong and courageous in raising my daughter. To my sons, because they were partly the ones who made her tough and who she mimicked after. To my mom, who has helped me from the beginning of my time and my daughter's life. To her friends, who love her unconditionally.

To the parents with special needs who sometimes feel alone, with no voice, but keep going. This is my encouragement to you. You are seen, you are noticed, and you have been heard by our Heavenly Father in Heaven. You also have a story to tell.

Contents

Foreword	1
Introduction	3
Chapter 1 Wait! It's not supposed to be this way!	5
Chapter 2 Feeling Guilty and Unattached	9
Chapter 3 Medevac in Survival Mode	13
Chapter 4 Becoming a Nurse Overnight	17
Chapter 5 Heart Surgery	21
Chapter 6 Miss Little Garden Island Crown	31
Chapter 7 Getting Ready for a Special Camp	39
Chapter 8 The Scary Detour From the Heart	43
Chapter 9 An Exhilarating Camp Experience	51
Chapter 10 Birthing a Bigger Community at Home	57

Chapter 11 I Hope you Dance	61
Chapter 12 Mariana's Missions	65
Chapter 13 Perfect Just the Way You Are	69
Chapter 14 Our Adventures in Traveling	75
Chapter 15 People Close To Her- Come and Gone	81
Chapter 16 Blessings in the Dark Valley	85
Chapter 17 Girls Bible Study	89
Chapter 18 Celebrations	95
Chapter 19 Our Time Together	101
Chapter 20 Her quiet spirit – Her Relationship with God	109
Chapter 21 It's Time to Dream Again	111
About The Author	115

Foreword

Ana wrote this book to help those in the special needs community, both known and unknown to her, to offer hope. She believes everyone has a story to share. She prays you will find the strength and courage to tell your story after reading hers.

Introduction

This is a love story of a baby girl born with Down syndrome. When I saw my little girl, I cried. My heart ached as I watched her struggle. As life unfolded, days and then years, passed by, many treasures were uncovered. I discovered that through all these trials, there were breakthroughs and barriers that came down. These wins were not just for me, but for others as well; to give encouragement and hope to those that are weary and feel alone.

I hope this story will help you discover your treasures in life and one day I will get to hear it. You have a voice!

Life is a circle of happiness, sadness, hard times, and good times. If you are going through hard times, have faith that good times are on the way.

– unknown

CHAPTER 1

Wait!
It's not supposed to be this way!

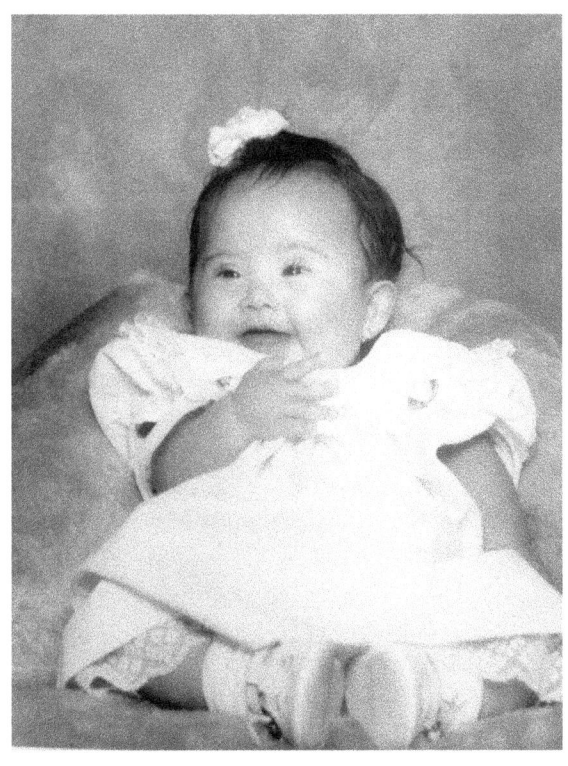

After a fast labor, my daughter was born four weeks early on September 6, 1996.

I noticed my birth coach, Poppy leaving the room for a few minutes. When she came back in, there were tears in her eyes. I had just given birth. I was relieved my baby was alright. Or was she?

The doctor said,

"You have a baby girl. Do you know what Down syndrome is?"

I couldn't understand the question. Why would he ask me that? I responded in a daze. I answered, "Yes."

Then he said, "Well, you have a baby with Down syndrome."

I couldn't remember anything else he said after that. I was in shock. There were many thoughts going through my head. One of those thoughts was, *No, for sure he misdiagnosed my daughter.*

Then I heard him say, "I will send you a pediatrician to explain more." Then, he left the room. I felt numb and cold from his words spoken to me.

Wait! It's not supposed to be this way!

When I heard the news, I started thinking about my mom. What would she think? What would she say? When my firstborn was born, she asked me, "Were all his fingers and toes there?" Now I had to tell her the news that I had what they call a Down syndrome baby, and I did not know how to take care of her. I was petrified!

The pediatrician, Dr. Bagnell, came in and said,

"Mrs. Munoz, she is a gift! Her face was lit up and full of compassion and excitement. You have a special child. What is her name? "Mariana," I responded faintly with a shattered heart.

Even though I felt the pediatrician meant every word she said, I still felt scared, shamed, and lost. How would my family react to this news? Would they treat me differently out of pity, or would I feel isolated and not understood?

Then it hit me. Overwhelmed by emotions, I cried. My birthing coach was trying to console me, and my daughter's pediatrician was trying to encourage me. My husband came a few hours later and saw my daughter and said,

"She's ours, and we will take good care of her."

When my mom heard the news, she didn't ask the same questions as she did with my firstborn. She said, "Ana, I will get better, and I will help you take care of her." My mom was going through chemo and radiation at that time. When I heard those words from my mom, I let out a sigh of relief. I felt that a ton of bricks had been taken off my back.

Growing up, I felt I was never good enough. I always felt I had to measure up, and I always wanted my mom to be proud of me.

I don't believe in coincidences, though I believe God connects the dots in our life. A few years ago, when my mom lived in California, she worked at an elementary school. In that school she helped take care of kids with special needs, specifically kids with Down syndrome. Little did I know that years later, she would have a grandchild with the same diagnosis.

Maybe, just maybe, I can get through this… this thought of hope peeked up in my head. I was about to discover my strength.

> *"Courage is resistance to fear, mastery of fear—not absence of fear." – Mark Twain*

CHAPTER 2

Feeling Guilty and Unattached

After coming to terms with her diagnosis, I felt unattached, guilty, and ashamed. My thoughts were, *I deserve this because I did not follow God the right way. He is punishing me.* I was also struggling with a secretive eating disorder, and I thought God was punishing me for committing that sin for many years.

When I was a teenager, I wanted to be like my other friends, skinny and pretty. Deep inside, I didn't feel I fit in. This disease started after my dad passed away. There was so much turmoil around me I couldn't control. But one thing I thought I could control was my body. This became a 10-year addiction. I finally got tired of hiding this secret and got some help from a Christian counselor. Even though I wasn't battling that eating disorder when my daughter was born, I was still struggling with guilt and shame. I didn't want to hold my baby because I felt depressed.

Going home with my new daughter was not a joyous time, but a stressful one. I would try to nurse her, and she would not latch on. I had to pump my breast because she wouldn't suck. Feelings of rejection were going through my mind. *I can't do this, God. Why?* I was getting more and more frustrated and scared. I would cry out to God out of desperation. Was he listening? Was God really listening? I felt alone and like a failure.

After the 4th day of Mariana not wanting to eat, I called the pediatrician. Mariana was pale, lethargic, and her lips were slightly blue. I described to her Mariana's symptoms. The pediatrician told me to bring her in. I took Mariana in right away.

They did some tests and found out she had an irregular heartbeat that was beating rapidly and had a loud murmur. After a thorough examination, she explained to me that I had to fly her to Oahu to do more testing, and that needed to be done that evening. The nurse made the arrangements quickly to get us to Oahu on an Air Ambulance. Questions were flooding through my mind. *How long would we have to stay away from home? Will she survive? Did I cause this to happen?*

Feeling Guilty and Unattached

During my pregnancy, I was working two jobs; at a helicopter company and at our new restaurant that we opened in July 1996. Once my daughter was born, I worked long hours at the restaurant. I wanted life to slow down, but I couldn't. Sometimes I felt I was like a hamster spinning around in this wheel. I felt I was on an emotional roller coaster and had no one to help process what I was feeling, except God.

There were many things I had to figure out before going to the hospital, with my eldest son and with the restaurant. I was stressed and emotionally distraught. I knew I had to latch on to God. He was the one I felt gave me strength.

My priorities were changing overnight. Going away from the business was a huge deal. I had to choose between the business, which was my livelihood, or my daughter's life. I felt guilty thinking this way. Having my firstborn, and the business, I thought I had things under control, but now with my daughter needing medical attention and having to go away with her by myself, I felt out of control and scared.

My oldest son was three years old at the time and would stay behind with his dad. He didn't understand the seriousness of what was happening, and that was okay. He just knew that mommy was going away for a while to help his little sister get well. I had to trust God. I had to believe this soon will pass… and hopefully get better.

The lesson I learned here was to trust and persevere because this little life was worth fighting for.

> *"It's important to know what really matters in life. Your sanity; your health; your family; and the ability to start anew."* – Les Brown

CHAPTER 3

Medevac in Survival Mode

I went away afraid to take care of my daughter and I still felt unattached and numb. Deep down inside, I felt God had started changing my heart. Could God be bonding me with my daughter through this hardship?

We flew to Kapiolani Hospital, in Oahu. When we arrived at the hospital that evening, the doctors and nurses went into high gear. They started doing all kinds of tests. They connected her to all these cables. The beeping sounds on the machines were going off. That kept my mind alert. I couldn't stand the sight of the nurses poking my daughter continuously because they couldn't find a good vein to put an IV in her. My heart was aching for her. Inside, I was crying out to God, *please make them stop*!

I was not numb anymore. My daughter was fighting for her life, and I wanted to help her, but I couldn't. I felt helpless. After a few more tests, the cardiologist discovered Mariana had an atrial ventricular septal defect and a tetralogy of fallot. In plain English, the way I understood it was that Mariana had two holes in her heart and one of her arteries needed to be repaired because it was blocking the flow of her heart. Heart surgery was needed.

"But when?" I asked.

I was so distraught! Surgery could not take place right away because she was too frail, and the doctor wanted her to grow bigger and stronger for the surgery.

I noticed something inside of me was shifting. It started here. God was bonding me to my daughter. I went from feeling numb to feeling like a roaring lioness wanting to save my little cub. From out of nowhere, I was feeling courageous! It came out of nowhere. Or did it?

We stayed at the hospital for two weeks. My friend Kim, who used to be my roommate at one time when I was living on the Big Island, had moved to Oahu, and offered me to stay in her home. She was so selfless and full of love. She committed to drive me back-and-forth to the hospital every day. Each day became more difficult for me. It wasn't so much the drive back and forth and seeing Mariana, that was hard. What was hard was the environment I was in. I could smell fear all around the neonatal floor. There was so much tension, I felt my adrenaline rushing through my veins like I was in survival mode. And I was in survival mode. In my mind, I had to fight that fear and anxiety every time I entered the room.

Late one evening, I got a call from the hospital. A nurse told me that Mariana's heart had gone into cardiac arrest but that they were doing everything possible to keep her alive. They reassured me they were monitoring her closely, but that she was in good hands. My heart dropped. I pondered, *Lord, why would you give me my daughter this way? I know you have a good plan for her. Tell me what to do.* Unexplainable, I felt this peace, and I went over to the hospital and started to pray over her by her side. I almost felt she felt me. I would start talking to her and cheering her on, telling her she was going to come out strong. I would whisper in her ear, "Mariana, you are strong and courageous!"

Every day, she was getting more stable with the meds they prescribed to her. I updated my family back home on Kauai, on every detail of Mariana's progress. I also kept checking up on my son Angel and the business. Knowing that things were okay over there, helped me feel a bit at ease.

After two weeks at the hospital, the cardiologist sent her home. He would schedule the heart surgery later, so she could gain more strength and be a few months older. I was informed that this surgery would take place in California at San Diego Children's Hospital. It is known as one of the best children's hospitals in the nation.

I was scared because I didn't know the outcome. Was this a test? And if it was, would I pass this test? This seemed like another mountain I needed to climb. I couldn't quit now.

What I was learning from this was, I had to release my fears to God. Even though I didn't know what was coming ahead, I knew He knew. I was also learning how important it was to hold on to peace, the peace that surpasses my understanding. I cannot buy this peace, but I can freely receive it from God. As the days passed, I kept saying to my daughter, let's keep going!

> *"Some of the best days of your life haven't happened yet. Keep going." – unknown*

CHAPTER 4

Becoming a Nurse Overnight

We departed from the hospital with instructions, medications, a nebulizer, and a stethoscope. I felt I had become a nurse overnight. I had to make sure that Mariana didn't turn blue around the lips, get clammy, or break into cold sweats. I barely slept, continuously checking up on her during the night, making sure she was breathing. A nurse was sent to my home once a week to make sure that Mariana and I were okay. My adrenaline was in overdrive.

A few weeks later, I got a call from Dr. Bagnell, the pediatrician. The surgery would be in six months. In the meantime, I had to make sure she was getting stronger. What was I doing to strengthen her? I was giving her my breast milk, her heart medicine, taking her to the doctor every two weeks, and I was praying to God for her.

Life felt a bit normal, I guess. I was getting used to my new routine. I would go to the restaurant on a weekly basis. I hired a nanny part-time to help me watch her at the restaurant. When things were slow, I would pump my milk in the back office so my nanny could feed her.

As months went by, my anxiety subsided. I was getting into a routine of monitoring her. The bonding had grown. My church community was always willing to give us a helping hand. But my mom could still not come because she was still going through her treatments of chemo and radiation. Even though my strength was building inside, I felt more comfortable to ask for help. It helped to know I didn't have to carry this load alone. I realized I was not alone.

My tiny girl was like a raggedy doll, flimsy and fragile. Her muscle tone was close to nonexistent. I started taking Mariana to Easter Seals Early Intervention Therapy once a week, which is a program for infants and toddlers with special needs. These services helped my daughter achieve cognitive, social, emotional, communicative, and physical development. It took place at a childcare facility close to home. These services made a significant impact for the first three years of my daughter's life.

The therapists were so compassionate. I could tell they loved doing their job. It helped me feel at ease and cared for. My daughter was in good hands. It was there that

I felt somewhat connected with other moms. My fear was subsiding as I was learning more and more about their unique stories and struggles.

The lesson I learned was I needed people around me that were walking the same journey I was on.

"Alone we can do so little, together we can do so much. There is strength in numbers." – unknown

CHAPTER 5

Heart Surgery

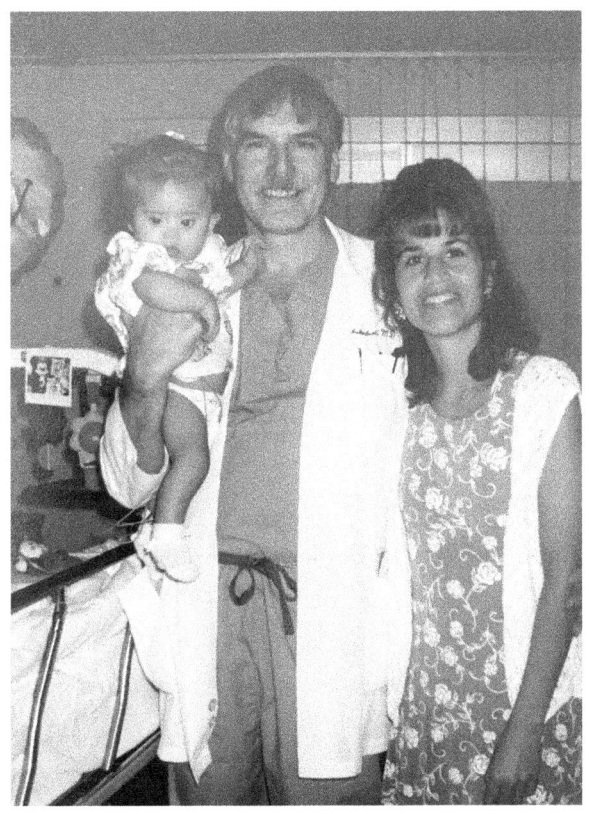

Perfectly Loved

I heard from Dr. Bagnell in Kauai, that this doctor was one of the best, Dr. Lamberti. That made me feel a bit at ease. The day in March 1997 came, and it was time for Mariana and I to go on a long, unknown journey. I felt anxious. As we were approaching San Diego, I noticed my daughter was having a hard time breathing. I called the hospital as soon as we arrived. The Doctor advised me to bring Mariana in right away. As soon as we got her to the hospital, she was admitted. She had developed pneumonia, so the doctors ordered more tests.

My heart was aching every time they would poke her little body. It was hard for them to find her veins because she was so puffy. I just wanted them to stop, but I knew it was necessary for her to get well. Her little eyes would look at me with desperation. She was such a good baby. She would barely cry, but every time they would poke her, she would start crying, something that was not normal for her to do. I knew she was in a lot of pain because while she was in the hospital, she cried alligator tears.

"Lord, please make them stop," I would cry out to God.

The doctor that attended to her was not very pleasant to deal with. They thought she had developed meningitis. So, they stuck a big needle in her spine. Thank God that the results came back negative. By this time, I thought I was going crazy! My mind was so emotionally drained that I thought any minute I would have a

Heart Surgery

nervous breakdown. My mom and aunt came to visit and that was such a relief. I gave myself permission to fall apart and cry.

Mariana stayed at the hospital for two weeks. The doctor and surgeon decided to postpone the surgery for the summer. We still had to stay close to the hospital for a few more days before heading back home. They had given her this medication that was so strong that it made her vomit and gave her diarrhea nonstop. I thought I was going to lose her! I called the cardiologist in Hawaii and told him about the urgent situation. I prayed and asked God to tell me what to do. The doctor said to give her a lesser dose so we could wean her off. I said, "Dr. I am taking her off this medication right away! I can't stand seeing my daughter shriveling up. She can't retain anything, not even water." I was shaking like a leaf full of fear. I took her off the meds and she slowly got her color and mild strength back. The vomiting and diarrhea completely stopped. I could feel this was truly a miracle!

A few months had gone by, and it was summer. The surgery was scheduled, and we were ready for round two. Mariana was chunkier and as healthy as she could be with her heart defect. We were going to stay at a hotel close by because the Ronald McDonald House was full. My mom stayed with me for support. She was in remission and felt strong enough to be by my side. That meant so much to me.

The night before her surgery, the surgeon called us and asked us if we could meet with him. He wanted to make sure that we understood the procedure. We met in the hotel lobby. He drew the pictures so well. It was important for him to know that we didn't have any questions. No wonder he was well known as one of the best surgeons in the country. They were going to enlarge one of her arteries and would also seal two holes in her heart. The surgery would take about eight hours.

"That's it, Doctor! We know you are one of the best and with God on your side, how could anything go wrong? Can we please pray for you?" My mom boldly asked. He humbly accepted.

The next morning, Mariana was wheeled in for surgery. I held her hand before going through those big swinging doors.

"Lord, please take care of her." I cried out in faith and hope.

The surgery was over eight hours later. Tubes were hanging out of her little body. She looked so puffy. They had to make sure all fluids were draining properly. It hurt me to see her little body bandaged and hooked up to machines. One thing the surgeon mentioned before surgery was that when they cut her open, they would cut her across a little below her chest. He explained that way when she grew up and wanted to wear a two-piece bathing suit, no one could see the scar from her surgery. I was so moved that he thought about her adolescent years in her future. I never would've thought that was an option. He won my heart and trust when he explained this part of the procedure with such care and detail in mind. I let out a sigh of relief and another silent prayer of hope and thanks,

"Thank you, Lord. I can see something good is going to happen."

The doctors released her after a month, and we flew back home with no complications. It was time to get readjusted to my son, my fragile daughter and the restaurant that was becoming very busy. I would still have a nurse check up on her for a few months. I also hired a lady from church to watch her at the restaurant while I was working for a few hours. It was working out quite smoothly. I would take my short breaks and would pump my breast milk. She would give her the bottle and I could keep an eye on her while I was working, in case we ran into any problems. We did this for a few months until we moved closer to the restaurant. My mom decided to rent her home in California and to move to Kauai so she could help me take care of Mariana. I was so appreciative.

Sixteen months later, I found out I was pregnant again. Some thoughts crossed my mind. *"What if"* thoughts.

I didn't entertain those thoughts very long. I was busy running the restaurant and taking care of my kids. My oldest son didn't see anything different with my daughter. He would play rough with her most of the time. He thought because he was tough, he could treat her the same. Well, the good thing was that Mariana learned to be tough as well. One day we were at the restaurant, and I had her car seat propped up on one of the tables while I was going to get something in the kitchen. Then I heard a bang!

My son accidentally knocked her off the table. She fell face first with the car seat on top of her. I ran to see what had happened. She wasn't breathing. I picked her up and put her in the back of the car and sped off to the hospital that was five minutes away. I started praying out loud for her to breathe. She let out a big scream, one that I had never heard before. I took her to emergency so they could examine her head, her brain, her nose, and her whole body. Nothing was broken. She only had a bruise on her nose.

"God, that was a miracle! Thank you, thank you, thank you!" I kept repeating. For sure, she had an angel watching over her.

My third child was born in June, and we opened our second restaurant that same month. Life became busier. I would bring both babies to the restaurant. I would have a crib in the office. The office was very cramped and tucked away in the back, past the kitchen. Our restaurants were voted #1 Best on the Island. We were working a lot of hours. We had good staff and often my kids would be at the restaurant for long hours as well. But most of the time, my mom would help me with my daughter for a few hours every day. I started feeling guilty that I was working more than taking care of my own kids. We basically lived at the restaurant. When it was slow, I would sometimes take them to the park, which was half a block away, and play with them. Though most times, the restaurant became their second home.

Mariana started preschool at age three. The first year was unbelievably stressful. Every week, she would get sick. Her immune system was very weak. I would constantly have to put her on antibiotics which I believed were bad, if taken too often. This went on for a couple of years. I felt so frustrated! Again, I prayed, "God, I need help. I need my daughter to stay healthy."

One day, my friend gave me a book about a mom who had a daughter with Down syndrome. In that book, there was some information about a supplement that the mom gave her daughter, and it helped her daughter's immune system get stronger. That wasn't the only benefit. It also helped her get rid of toxins from her body.

Mariana wasn't too chubby, but she was puffy and that was because her body retained a lot of toxins. I started researching about that supplement but was unsuccessful in finding out what it was. A few weeks after, the county fair came into town. They had different booths with vendors. Well, lo-and-behold, I couldn't believe my eyes! I saw this man selling a product and right next to it was the book I had just read.

"Oh, my gosh!" I yelled.

"I want that product!" I told the vendor as I approached the table. He looked puzzled by my reaction.

"Do you know about this product?" He asked.

"Well, no. But I read that book," pointing to the exact book I had read a few weeks before. I continued, "And if that supplement gave good results to that girl, I know it will do the same for my daughter."

He then wanted to meet with me and explain more details about it. We met the next day at my restaurant and he said,

"I would love to meet your daughter."

He met my daughter and his eyes welled up.

Heart Surgery

He said with excitement, "I can't wait until Mariana takes this supplement."

I started my daughter on these supplements and started noticing changes in a matter of two weeks. I called my new friend up and told him the positive results. Mariana wasn't sick for those two weeks. I noticed she was more energetic and processing information quicker. I told him that in a few weeks she was going to compete in a county race from the elementary school and he could meet us there. This race was not a Special Olympics race, this was a school race that the county had put on.

"On your mark, get set, go!" Mariana ran fast! She was coordinated and even though she did not win, she finished the race. She was celebrated because she was the only child with Down syndrome that had entered this race on this island. My heart leaped with pride and joy. I looked over at my new friend and he had tears in his eyes. He told me he knew this supplement worked, but he had never seen it firsthand with someone who was with Down syndrome. "Wow", I said.

"Well, now you convinced me." To this day, Mariana still takes this supplement. It has helped her stay healthy. My lesson learned here was to stay attentive to new opportunities and new friendships, because this one was an answer to prayer for better health.

"Hope is important because it can make the present moment less difficult to bear. If we believe that tomorrow will be better, we can bear a hardship today." – Thich Nhat Hanh.

CHAPTER 6

Miss Little Garden Island Crown

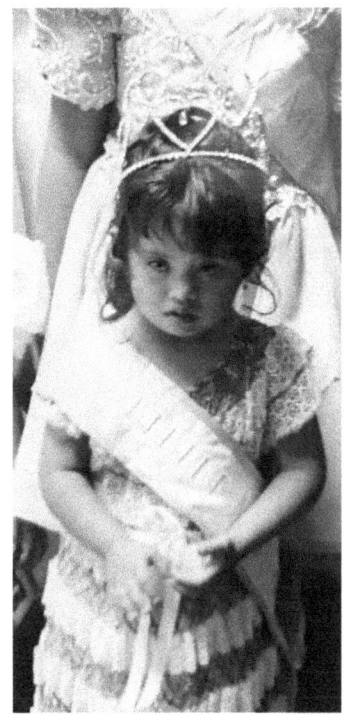

My good friend, Stacey, was putting her daughter in a beauty pageant and tried to convince me to enter Mariana as well. I declined the first couple of times she asked me. She saw something in Mariana that I didn't see in her yet. So, the more I thought about it, the more I reconsidered.

"Well, why not? She would only need to do a talent, show a sport outfit and a gown." That didn't seem so hard.

Perfectly Loved

"Ok, we'll do it!" I told my friend Stacey. Mariana was 5 years old.

I had put her in gymnastics a few months before that. Her coach Lisa was so amazing with her. She was gentle, she was loving, patient and understanding. She had a couple more students with special needs, and that made me feel comfortable in signing her up to these classes. I was thrilled when I found out about those particular classes. She loved to swing and tumble. She was also good at mimicking the others that were in front of her. Mariana blended very well with her gymnastic peers. I learned she was very limber. She could do the splits and stretch all the way to the ground like it was not hurtful or strenuous for her.

Once I committed to entering Mariana in the beauty pageant, I asked her coach if she would teach her a routine so she could show that as her talent at the pageant. Her gymnastics coach was so excited to do so. Mariana worked hard to learn the routine. Just like everybody else, she learned by repetition, but at a slower pace. Her coach was so patient with her. Sometimes Mariana just wanted to play and would make her coach chase her. It was quite trying, but entertaining to watch. Inside my heart I would pray, *please don't let her give up on my daughter.*

When I signed Mariana up to this pageant, I didn't tell them she was special needs. In the back of my mind,

I was afraid she would be rejected for being special needs. But they were very kind and surprised when I entered her. They asked me what her talent would be, and I responded,

"Gymnastics."

Her coach was amazing and one of a kind. She went above and beyond coaching her. For the pageant, she brought the bars on stage for Mariana's simple routine. Mariana went confidently on stage and did some tumbling and hanging on the bars. She spun around like a ballerina, smiled, and walked off the stage. Her outfit was designed and tailored by a friend of mine. All I had to do was bring her a Barbie doll outfit, and she copied it in Mariana's size.

It was a long day at the pageant from morning to late afternoon. The different updo's for all three categories, the make-up and the change of outfits were time-consuming. I could see Mariana was getting flustered.

I was relieved once they announced the winners. Mariana got third place in her age category. I was so overjoyed! Even though putting her in a beauty pageant was not on my bucket list, I felt it should've been. It was the beginning of breaking down barriers out of the social norm.

Perfectly Loved

One year had passed, and I figured that chapter was done until my friend Stacey approached me again and encouraged me to enter Mariana again in another pageant.

Mariana had been learning Hula and Sign Dance through our church. She loved music; that I knew. I felt maybe she could learn a Hula song specifically for the pageant. I reached out to another friend from church, and she taught Mariana this special song, 'Show me your Way' by Darlene Zschech. It was a beautiful song.

I remember that before she got on stage, I prayed for her, saying, "Ok Lord, do what you do best. Use her for your Glory. She is yours!"

And I sent her off on stage. My tiny little girl got on that stage, and you could hear a pin drop. All eyes in the audience were on her. Mariana danced her hula, and I looked all around the audience. There were people crying. In my mind I was thinking, *why are they crying?* I suddenly felt this unexplainable peace. She did every motion of the song and got off the stage. I looked over at the judges, and one had teary eyes. I was so relieved that Mariana had done so well. The rest of the pageant was easy.

Now it was time to announce the winners. The judges had made their decision. I didn't know if she was going to place. There were a lot of pretty contestants with great talents. But I knew I did the right thing. I had entered Mariana in the pageant to expose her ability. She was a gift from God, and I knew something great was going to come out of this even if she didn't win.

The 3rd runner-up…
I thought, *well, even if she didn't place, I know I did the right thing.*

The 2nd runner-up …
I thought, *well I'm sad that she didn't place.* There were a lot of good talented girls and more experienced.

The 1st runner-up…
Ok, well Lord, I know you are going to use this for good in some way or another, were my thoughts.

And the winner of Miss Little Garden Island is… Mariana Muñoz!!

Wait, what! Did I hear right? I started bawling. Each one of those tears was an expression of joy and the realization that she was validated. The trophy that was given to her was as big as her. And even though she didn't realize the true meaning of this pageant, I knew, and other people knew. This was the beginning of a new breakthrough in our community, and she was being celebrated!

That year, there were many parades that took place on the island where she would get to dress up and all she had to do was do the princess wave to the public. That was loads of fun. My boys got to be in the convertible cars a couple of times and throw candies into the crowds. I would see the people's faces with amazement and delight, cheering, as they would see my daughter who had Down syndrome, pass by, and she was included in each of the big events celebrated by the community.

There was a lady reporter who wanted to do a story about Mariana and our family. In the story, I gave God the credit. My daughter was a survivor, the one who was a touch and go at one time because of her heart defect. I believe God played a big part. Mariana, being a fighter, was breaking through something others hadn't tried before. It was a very busy year for us. I believe through this amazing experience, the restaurant got even more popular.

Then came the day when she had to give away her title as Miss Little Garden Island. She had to show a talent. I taught her some sign dance moves to a song named, "I hope you dance" by Lee Ann Womack. The reason I picked this song for her was because at one time I did not know if she would survive when she was fighting for her life. These obstacles have strengthened her. I thought, *'Yes, she will continue to dance in life.'*

I learned from this experience to not be afraid of being the first to break through a barrier. The blessings we got were overflowing!

> *"Today, many will break through the barriers of the past by looking at the blessings of the present. Why not you?" – Steve Maraboli*

CHAPTER 7

Getting Ready for a Special Camp

My two boys would always attend a summer camp every year. I would feel sad because I wanted Mariana to attend camp as well. Unfortunately, that was not offered locally, but I would pray that one day Mariana could attend a camp.

I didn't want my daughter to experience the rejection I once felt. A few years back, I took my daughter and my youngest son to a five-day club and that turned out to be a hurtful experience. After I dropped them off, I got a call from the director one hour later, asking me if I could pick up my daughter from the club because they were not staffed to take care of her. My heart was broken. I felt the rejection, and it cut me deep. My feelings surrounding fear and rejection surfaced as I thought of the day my daughter was born. Then I thought, "It's one thing for me to be rejected, but now my daughter?" I went over there crying and gave her a piece of my wounded heart. I picked up both of my kids and left.

That same day, I found another day camp at another church. It was a five-day Bible Club. I went there crying. I shared with them what had just happened, and they gladly wanted to take my daughter in. They accepted her with open arms.

At that moment, I could feel God's love through those people at that church.

Getting Ready for a Special Camp

I did not want an awful experience repeated. It was too painful. My prayer became more intentional.

"Lord, would you bring a camp for my daughter? I want Mariana to experience camp like my boys can."

Soon after, my friend told me that her daughter, Shealynna was going to volunteer at a summer camp that was for special needs. The camp would take place in Arizona, and it would be for a week. My heart leaped with excitement. I researched it and got hold of the area director, David Thames in Phoenix, Arizona. Mariana was thirteen years old and attending 8th grade. The camp was for ages 14-21-year-olds. After talking to the director, he told me that since it was so close to her birthday that he would accept her. There were a few things that needed to happen. I would need to be her chaperone, and we would need to come up with $1100 for camp. That did not include the flight. I thought, okay God, I believe this was an answer to a prayer, so my next prayer was,

"Help us raise that money to go to camp."

We had to raise funds for the flight and the camp. It was pricey for both of us, but I was committed to making it happen. I did a fundraiser, and the area coordinator had told me they would include Mariana in their fundraisers as well. *'Wow!'* I thought, this would be a miracle if we pulled it off. The camp was in July. So, we had about four months to fundraise. The director told us he would help us raise some funds at their end. Is this really happening? I was so overjoyed! Thank you, Lord! Another miracle for the books!

The lesson from this chapter was to dream big in life and speak it out until you believe it and see it.

"A dream becomes a goal when action is taken toward its achievement." – Bo Bennett

CHAPTER 8

The Scary Detour From the Heart

I noticed Mariana was lacking energy. Her teacher mentioned to me that she would constantly put her head down on her desk at school during class and didn't seem to have any energy. They asked me if she was getting enough sleep at night. I would answer, "Yes." even though she liked to stay up late with her dad when he'd come home from work, which was 11 PM.

One morning, I woke her up to go to school, and I noticed when she went downstairs that she was perspiring and was turning blue and unresponsive. It was almost like she was in a daze. I immediately started praying for her and commanded her valve in her heart to open in Jesus' name. Those were the words that immediately came out of my mouth to speak out. Suddenly, her color came back to normal. I was concerned and shocked at that unexplainable miracle. *Wow Lord, what do you want me to do now?* I thought.

I told the teacher that morning to please keep a close eye on her. That day, I made an appointment with her doctor. The doctor, in turn, made an appointment with the cardiologist from Oahu. He flew to Kauai a few days later. He did an EKG, which is a monitor that reads her heart, and he noticed something abnormal and said,

"Mrs. Munoz, how fast can you get on a flight to San Diego?"

The Scary Detour From the Heart

I didn't really get why he was asking me that question. I answered with a puzzled look.

"Why?"

He answered, "because your daughter has had episodes of tachycardia, which is when the heart races and her heart could stop at any minute. We need to correct this as soon as possible. We may have to put a pacemaker in her."

I was in a state of shock. I did not want to accept the bad news.

I whispered, "I rebuke that in the name of Jesus. I will not agree with the bad news." God had given me peace, and I felt He had a plan.

This happened three months before camp. I notified the area director of the camp right away, and they immediately started to pray for Mariana. I didn't have time to be exhausted. I did not have time to be scared. It was time for battle in faith for my daughter.

We got on the plane and checked into the Ronald McDonald House at San Diego's Children's Hospital a couple of days later. I met the cardiologist the next day at the hospital. He explained Mariana had to have a pacemaker. I told him I did not have peace about her getting a pacemaker because her body was so tiny that the device would pop out and may cause problems. I informed many people before leaving Kauai of this urgency. Plenty of people from all over the world started praying for my daughter. They were people from an orphanage, from Christian schools, from churches, from home group and prayer groups. They all started praying for Mariana. My oldest son sent a prayer request to his friend that was leading an orphanage in Mexico. He texted my son back right away, and he said,

"Mariana will get healed. Not only that, but she will even get to go to the zoo after. Right away, I felt a jolt in my heart of excitement and hope. I felt God was waking up my faith. I said out loud,

"OK Lord, I receive that word in Jesus' name." It was time to war in prayer. This lifted up my spirit.

One day before surgery, I cried out to the Lord with these words.

"Lord, you know my heart and I don't have peace about the doctors inserting that pacemaker in her little chest."

I felt the Lord tell me, "Watch what I'm about to do. I am never late. Just trust me."

The Scary Detour From the Heart

Wow, I thought. *I want to believe in a miracle. Help my unbelief.*

When one of my sisters heard about my daughter needing surgery, she sent me a video of this preacher that shared on how to believe in everyday miracles. I watched this video about five times repeatedly. Watching this video over and over helped me expand my faith. I noticed fear and unbelief melt away. My faith was about to be tested.

As they were preparing her to go into surgery, the cardiologist took me aside and said to me,

"Mrs. Munoz, something strange happened last night. I woke up at 3 AM this morning thinking about your daughter. I don't think that we will put a pacemaker in her, but we will try to do something else. We will try to insert a defibrillator in her heart. That way it will not show outside of her little body."

He explained what it was, which is a small battery-powered device placed in the chest to detect and stop irregular heartbeats (arrhythmias). It would continuously monitor the heartbeat and would send electric shocks, when needed, to restore a regular heartbeat. Then he proceeded to roll her in.

Four hours had gone by and no word. I was getting anxious and scared. But then I would remind myself,

God's got this. I kept praying, and I knew more people all over the world were praying for Mariana as well. Six hours later, the surgeon came out and said,

"Okay, she's done."
I asked, "What did you do to her?"

He said, "We couldn't do anything. We tried to stress her heart, and it was beating normal. We can't explain what happened."

They couldn't proceed with implanting the device because they couldn't stress her little heart. "Like I said, I can't explain it!" he said with a puzzled look.

I responded, "I can Doctor. God touched her heart!"

I thanked him with my eyes filled with tears of joy. I immediately texted my oldest son to let his school know that Mariana didn't need the surgery after all and that we had just witnessed a miracle. I later heard that when the kids at school heard the news, they were jumping up and down and some of them were even crying tears of joy and praising God.

The Doctors told me that Mariana needed to stay at the hospital for observation and then after four weeks we could go home. Three weeks went by, and we had made friends with different people in the Ronald McDonald

House. Some patients had terminal illnesses. One was getting chemo, and I prayed for God to give him strength. I remember a parent asked me, "How can you stay at peace in the middle of turmoil?" I got to share with her my relationship with God and explained that's who gave me peace.

One day, the cardiologist's secretary had asked me if I was interested in taking Mariana to San Diego Sea World. I was so elated! Remember the prayer my son's friend said? He said,

"I pray Mariana will get healed and not only that, but she will also go to the zoo."

Well, there you go! That prayer was about to be answered. I was so amazed how much God loves us. At that moment, I felt he was showering us with His love.

The secretary got us a shuttle and took us to Sea World one Sunday morning. We were in the park until they closed. One ride Mariana wanted to go on was *The Atlantis*. She was barely tall enough. I said a prayer before getting on. "Lord, I believe you healed her, and I want to thank you for protecting her on this ride." Up we went and down the slopes, ending with a gush of water on us. The look on her face said everything! Mariana had a blast on that roller coaster. She was smiling from ear to ear. She got to climb on the jungle gym bars in the playground and she got to see many live animals. We got to see penguins, fish, birds, turtles, seals, and whales. That was our kind of zoo! That day was priceless.

The lesson I learned was faith. My faith became stronger after going through this journey.

> *"Prayer is not asking. Prayer is putting oneself in the hands of God, at His disposition, and listening to His voice in the depth of our hearts."*
>
> *– Mother Teresa*

CHAPTER 9

An Exhilarating Camp Experience

Perfectly Loved

After the big heart scare and with her doctor's approval, I could now plan for Mariana's first camp in July. The camp was going to take place in Arizona. I had never been to Arizona before and now it was an opportunity to go to a beautiful area called Flagstaff, where the camp for special needs would take place for a week. All we had to do was to book a flight.

I was so blessed to have my daughter experience a special camp tailored for her. I was nervous because I didn't know any of the people, except for phone conversations I had with the area director. There were live videos that we were required to attend, but that was it. It was July first, and we got to the Arizona airport around 5:30 AM. It was a long, hot, grueling day. We had to wait until the last flight would come in, which was about 11 AM, so we could all get on the bus and head to the campgrounds. When we got to the campgrounds, they had a welcome party. Well, Mariana and I were already ready to turn in. We were exhausted from the long journey. We had been traveling since the night before. We were kindly excused on the first day.

The next few days were exhilarating, energetic and unforgettable. There were lots of outdoor games, skits, great food, talent shows, competitions, inspirational messages, dancing, water activities, zip lining, pool parties and so much more!

An Exhilarating Camp Experience

Mariana and I got to experience the zip lining, which landed in the water. At first Mariana did not want to go up. She fears some heights, not all heights, though. Some of those height fears are walking over a bridge, the Ferris wheel, and the scaffold that was taking us up to the zip line. Once she was buckled in and the staff reassured her she was going to be ok, she was fine. What was fun was that one landed on water. The staff made a video that they showed the last day at camp. They caught Mariana zip lining all the way down. It showed she was having the best time of her life.

On a different day, we went on a giant swing where there would be three people seated together. They would pull you up and you would have to unhook yourself from the rope so the swing would come down; and boy, it swung full force! At first, I was scared going on it. I think this was Mariana's favorite ride.

On the last night of the camp, there was a talent show. They highly recommended each team to do a talent. There was a song that Mariana and I had performed at church together, doing creative sign dance. We didn't have a team that we came with, so it was just the two of us. We practiced it a couple times, and I volunteered to perform the last night on stage in front of 500 people. Mariana did so well. She remembered all her moves. Afterwards, people came up to us to thank us for doing that creative sign dance. One of them was deaf, and he was deeply touched by it. It was very moving for me that a simple song together would touch people's hearts. Definitely, God was using her in a special way.

At camp, I met the founding president of the organization, Nick Palermo. I told him I would love to bring something like this camp to Kauai. He stopped and listened and told me,

"Ana, you get me ten students and I'll come down and help you start a monthly club so we can get you geared to doing a summer camp next summer."

When I got home, I started spreading the word about clubs and camps. The only thing they had available that I knew of was the Special Olympics. All the parents I talked to were very excited to hear about the upcoming plans. I made flyers and gave out information about our first club.

We got many volunteers together and started planning our new experience. So, on September 11, 2010, we started our club with twelve students and a few high school volunteers. The founding president of the organization, Nick, flew down to help start it, and our goal was to have a club once a month. We would have a theme for every club. Some themes were: favorite hero, your favorite color, athlete theme, Easter theme, Bible character theme and Christmas theme. We would

An Exhilarating Camp Experience

include food, a craft, a game, an inspirational message from the Bible and end with a dance. Then we would send them off with a flyer for our next event. This event club was the buzz of the town. *The Garden Island Newspaper* wrote about us. Now, our next step was our local camp for our special needs community. Hooray!

The lesson I learned from this experience was don't be afraid to try new things in life.

> *"Too many people are thinking of security instead of opportunity. They seem to be more afraid of life than death."*
>
> *– James F. Byrnes*

CHAPTER 10

Birthing a Bigger Community at Home

My oldest son used to go to a private school up in the mountains. It was very nice, quite peaceful and with an amazing view of the mountains. In the summer, the property was vacant. I had an idea! Why couldn't we have a camp on this property? The property had a certified kitchen, assembly room, a gym, and some cabins. I immediately called the property manager and asked her what it would cost for us to use the facilities? And if it was available for us to use the facilities in June? I explained to her what the program was all about. The price was unbeatable, and the place was available. Wow! I called the founding president of the nonprofit organization, and he came a month later to scout the property. I felt like God had opened this place just for us. Nick, the founding president, was dumbfounded when he saw the property. He said, "Wow, Ana this place would be perfect for camp. Now, we need to nail down the specifics."

We started doing a couple of fundraisers. One was making mini pumpkin pies and selling them. We had amazing volunteers that had a great and tasty recipe. Everyone who bought them loved them! It beat selling donuts or doing a car wash.

Our Concert Fundraiser

Our next fundraiser was a concert. In this concert one of my friends on the mainland had a business setting up concerts. Her husband called one of their buddies in a band that was already scheduled to do a gig in Maui and volunteered his time to come and play for us for our fundraising concert. We added a local high school band called the Buddy System to play at the event. They were also abundant volunteers with this organization. We got the VIPs to make pottery a few weeks before our fundraiser so they could auction off their work of art during the concert. I also went to different business owners and told them about our upcoming event. Many were thrilled to donate their activities and products. The event took place at a Veterans Center. The price was discounted because there was one friend who was a Veteran that vouched for us so we could get a special price. I also got asked to speak on a famous local radio station and they played a couple of the songs from this group that were coming to play for us. My friend, who puts on the concerts, was giving me all the details on what needed to be done before the event. There was *The Garden Island Newspaper* reporter that came to-do a story on us.

The venue was filled. We had volunteers bring chili and rice, hot dogs, and baked goods to sell. So many volunteers pulled together. The concert was a success! We raised enough funds and then some for our camp.

I had another idea! How about if three out of the five days we take our campers on a different excursion? The other two days, we could do crafts and fun skits.

Day 1. We could use the YMCA pool and play games while having lunch.

Day 2. We could go to the Smith's Tropical Gardens, do a mini tour and have lunch.
Day 3. We could go to the Beach and have a picnic.

Nick loved the idea! The next thing was transportation. I set up a meeting with the mayor and he helped me make the arrangements with the County Bus Department. The Department of Transportation came to each property to assess the location since it wasn't a regular route. They accepted my request for the five days of camp. The pickup point would take place at our local church each day. Every morning, they would drop them off at the designated area where we were going to have the camp for the day. On the last day, we had a slideshow of all the amazing fun activities and excursions we went on, and we invited family and friends. Our ministry started growing. It was a hit!

On to the next big thing, but I didn't know what it was yet.

"First, I prepare. Then I have faith."
– Joe Namath

CHAPTER 11

I Hope you Dance

My daughter had never attended a school prom, and I wanted her to experience that. I called up my friend in Arizona, David, who had come out to help at our first camp. I started picking his brain about the proms he was creating in his hometown. I was looking at some pictures on social media about some groups of this nonprofit that were having their own prom. I thought, *Okay, why not have our own prom and have escorts by able peers, where they would be celebrated and treated as VIPs the whole night?*

I started talking to a friend who was the manager of a hotel. I was envisioning having this special prom at this hotel. This had never been done before. I told her about my vision and my mission. I wanted these VIPs special needs to experience a prom here on our Island that they would never forget. My friend was so excited and immediately came on board with my mission. We would just have to come up with the money for the food. The hotel donated the venue. Wow, what a gift!

Now I had to make a few more calls and have a few meetings with some great influencers on the Island. I told my team about it, and they were very excited. I felt God was moving in our favor. I set up a meeting with our Mayor again. He would be our special guest and speak a few words of encouragement. I spoke with the Department of Transportation and made special arrangements for pickup and drop offs. We had a newspaper reporter that wanted to attend and write a story on us. He said he wouldn't want to miss this for the world. We started asking some people in our church group if they would like to volunteer. Some volunteers were to do hair and make-up. I envisioned the girls getting a mini spa before the main event. I had the food bank bring some snacks and juice while they were waiting to get their up-do's and make up. We had so many volunteers that I had to turn some volunteers away.

Most of these ladies had never experienced this royal treatment. The parents would come in to drop off their daughters and they didn't want to leave. They were watching with amazement. They couldn't understand why we were doing this with so much love and excellence.

We had a special video made with interviews during the prom by some volunteers, VIPs and the Kauai Mayor. The total number of people, including the volunteers, was 85 people. All we had to come up with was 10.00 for each guest. Everything else was covered by donations and a couple of fundraisers.

Our night was full of excitement and anticipation. As the VIPS would walk in through the red carpet and a balloon arch, each one was announced on the microphone. They all had assigned seating with a head host. As they all settled in, the program started with a few singers, hula dancers and creative sign dance performance from a few girls with special needs. The seating was limited, so the parents would have to wait in the foyer with some appetizers while the VIPs were having a 3-course elegant meal. The Mayor got up to say a few words of encouragement and sang a fun song. After our dinner and performances, our DJ, who was my youngest son, started the music with an amazing playlist for everyone to dance to. Everyone glowed and celebrated. No one wanted that night to end. People were talking about it all year. And parents were so excited they were looking forward to the next year.

"We dance for laughter, we dance for tears, we dance for madness, we dance for fears, we dance for hopes, we dance for screams, we are the dancers, we create the dreams."

– Albert Einstein

CHAPTER 12

Mariana's Missions

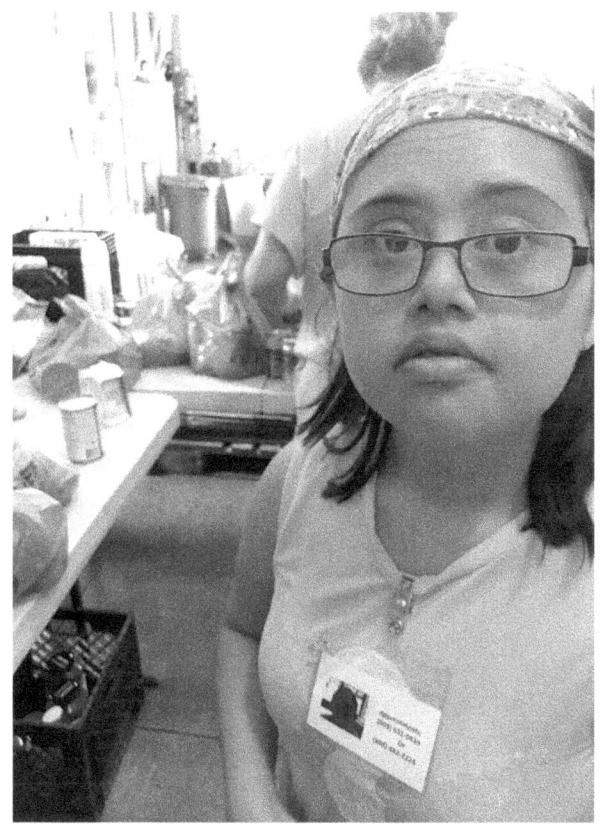

Perfectly Loved

Mariana loves children. When she was a little girl, I sometimes would go upstairs to her room, and would find a bunch of dolls lined up with a book in front of each of them. She pretended to be their teacher. She would entertain herself for hours in her room. I always thought she could be a good teacher someday.

In 2019, Mariana and I were going to go on a mission trip to the Dominican Republic, but then the pandemic hit, and that plan came to a halt. I was so excited to have her experience that journey in her life. My friend who is from the Dominican Republic, goes every year to help put together a Bible Summer Camp for the kids around Santo Domingo. I am confident that one day that journey will come to pass, but until then Mariana has done many missions here, where she lives.

Mariana loves the elderly. Every day she helps me take care of her 95-year-old grandma. She'll try to boss her around at times and at the same time, she shows her deep compassion. When she was about 10 years old, she would go with my mom and a group from my mom's church to visit the elderly people at the hospital every week. They would sing and if they wanted to be prayed for, my daughter would lay her hands on them and pray for them as well. Mariana enjoyed singing together with that group.

Mariana's Missions

Mariana also used to volunteer at the library weekly. We would clean the DVDs and put them in order.

A few years ago, Mariana and I would pay weekly visits to an assisted living care home. We would do puzzles with them or color with them and watch tv with them. She enjoyed visiting them and the residents would cheer up when they would see her.

There have been many times that my special needs group has performed for the elderly, a few songs with creative sign dance. Mariana has also performed in different events. Some have been in hospitals, care homes, churches, camps, their monthly Able Club and their yearly Special Prom. They love to be a part of something and want to feel they are making a difference in people's lives.

Mariana loves volunteering. During the pandemic, there was a non-profit organization that started delivering healthy organic foods to the elderly once a week. Mariana is still helping deliver food to this day, three years later.

Mariana also volunteered at the Hawaii Food Bank for over four years. We would go once a week for an hour and tidy up the cans and or sort out the bread that would come in from different stores. She didn't like it if anyone tried to do her job. She was focused and knew what she was supposed to do, and she took ownership and was very proud of herself that she could accomplish this type of job successfully.

The lesson from this is showing Mariana the principle of giving. When you give, you receive, and it is better to give than to receive.

It's better to give than to receive.
– Acts 20:35

CHAPTER 13

Perfect Just the Way You Are

Mariana resembled my mom when she was two years old. She has brown eyes and brown hair. She's very different from her brothers because both of her brothers have light eyes. When she was born, her hair was sticking up like someone had put their finger in an electric socket. She was cross-eyed, but thankfully, her eyes corrected themselves a few months later. She had a pudgy belly and would easily jolt at any kind of sudden movement around her.

Mariana was my easiest to raise. She's very organized. She loves routine. She's compassionate. She's bilingual, but chooses to speak English. Even though her speech is very limited, she can understand everything. When she doesn't understand, she will say, 'No', because she is trying to process the information and because she's a creature of habit. Mariana doesn't like change. But who does right?

She stays on task. She's a check off list kind of girl. I have a monthly calendar where I write her chores to do daily. Once the month runs out, she wants me to fill up more chores for the next month. I don't really have to remind her of her schedule because she has it all in her calendar. She loves to get things accomplished.

Mariana loves to look at pictures, call her friends or brothers on her phone or iPad. She likes to swim and shop. She always has a best friend she clings on to. Some of them have been her teachers. One of them has been a great friend over the years.

Mariana does not like me taking pictures of her. She hides her face. I trick her by telling her it is for one of her friends. Her favorite foods are rice, beans, tacos, chili, pizza, and spaghetti. She's not a picky eater. To my surprise, she does not eat too many sweets, but her favorite chocolate is Reese's Cups.

Mariana likes to cook. Every week when we have a girls' Bible study, I prepare food for the girls who attend our weekly Bible study. We keep the menu simple. Mostly spaghetti or chili and rice accompanied by a salad. Mariana oversees preparing the salad. She is very coordinated with the knife. She will cut the lettuce, dice the tomatoes, cucumbers, and carrots. She will then add some cheese and dice some turkey slices and mix it in. That is her job, and she doesn't want anyone to help her.

When we had the restaurant, Mariana loved to clean menus and put salsa in the little side dishes. It was for all our clients that would dine in. Sometimes she would get enough courage to serve the chips and salsa to our customers.

Mariana is very studious. She loves spending time in the library and pick out some books with lots of pictures. She will make up her own stories while looking at the pictures in the books.

Mariana is very independent. She does things like clockwork. She loves routines. For example, in the morning, she'll come into my room and pick up her electronic devices, her phone and her iPad. She'll lock herself in her room and call her friend to say, "Hi". Then she'll make a smoothie for grandma. She'll spend quiet time looking at pictures on her iPad and then start with some of her house chores.

She likes to do things around the house. It makes her feel purposeful. Some things she does around the house are laundry, vacuuming, watering plants and cleaning mirrors. Once she gets each chore done, she likes to check them off and go to the next one. She's a very tidy girl when it comes to personal hygiene. She will always take two showers a day. So that means more laundry to do. Gosh! She loves clothes. Every week she loves going to *Ross* and looking at girls' clothes. She has a lot of clothes. Once a year I will donate some of her clothes to secondhand stores. Her favorite color is pink. Even if you didn't know her, you could guess that was her favorite color.

We celebrate every small step in her life, from when she would hold her bottle to when she would say mommy. Her brothers would help a lot. I would say they were good teachers. She started sitting on her own when she turned one-year-old. The way she would get around was rolling around or walking on all fours, like a cute little monkey. She was very observant. She copied her brothers a lot. I saw her blossom more when my youngest was born. She mimicked everything he did. They were best buddies when they were both babies.

Perfect Just the Way You Are

They got potty trained together, and that was a big celebration for us. Diapers can get expensive!

We would always have big birthday parties for our kids. We had a big yard so we could rent water slides or have outdoor movie nights or picnics and invite the whole neighborhood friends. We would have talent shows and games with prizes. Everyone in the neighborhood and friends from church and school loved coming over to our parties. We would cook food from the restaurant and bring it over. Mariana loved to eat Mexican food. Her favorite is rice, beans and chicken. Every day after school, the bus driver would drop her off at the restaurant and she would walk in like she owned the restaurant. She would go right into the kitchen and ask for the same thing: "rice, beans, and chicken in a bowl, please". Sometimes, when it was closing time at the restaurant, I would bring my kids with me. We would turn off the lights and we would chase each other around. I loved playing with them. Mariana loves playing with her brothers as well. Sometimes we would have pillow fights in the living room. We had a lot of pillows on our 9-foot-long sofa. That was loads of fun! She didn't like it so much because sometimes the boys would throw the pillows a bit hard.

Something I learned from Mariana is don't forget to capture every moment and take time to play.

Perfectly Loved

"It's not about "having" time.
It's about making time."

– MAKE TIME

CHAPTER 14

Our Adventures in Traveling

Every year we would go on an adventure trip vacation. It was almost like going on a treasure hunt. I would always pick new places to explore. My kids would try to guess where we were going next. They always knew it was going to be loads of fun. Mariana was always an easy traveler.

I loved to travel with my kids because it was a time of experiencing the world. One of their teachers would comment, "Ana, where are you going this time? Can't wait to hear about your next adventure when you get back. Show us pictures because I want to see where I can go on my trip with my family next year!"

So, sure enough, one of Mariana's teachers got to experience one place we had traveled to after I shared our pictures with her. During each trip, we would take a lot of pictures and develop them. I would make a scrapbook together with Mariana so she could show her friends and teachers at school.

One time we went on the Disney Cruise. Even though it was a long trip, it was worth it! We got to stop at their private Disney Island, which it's called the Disney Castaway Island, in the Bahamas. There, we saw anchored offshore, the ship from the movie *Pirates of the Caribbean*. We had just seen the movie, so it added more excitement to seeing it in person.

Our longest trip was on a train from California to Ontario, Canada. And this time it was going to be from the plane to a train. I wanted Mariana and my boys to learn from every traveling experience. Our fun would start once we got on the plane. At take-off, Mariana would lift her arms in the air as if she was on a roller coaster.

Mariana loves to ride roller coasters. When we arrived in San Diego, we went to Sea World. She would want to get on the biggest roller coaster. The problem was that she wasn't tall enough to ride it. I was sometimes

Our Adventures in Traveling

relieved of that, since she was braver than me. We went on some good fun ones, though. We were there from opening to closing. We visited a good Mexican Restaurant and walked around all the shops in Old Town San Diego. The next day, we took a light rail and Amtrak train from Los Angeles to Colorado. Once we got to Colorado, we hit the mall and bought some souvenirs.

Mariana loved the train. We would always take our trips when it was the slow tourist season in Hawaii. They were the months of February or October. Mariana has been quite a traveler. She's gone to all the islands of Hawaii, California, Arizona, Colorado, Ohio, Maryland, Virginia, DC, Florida, New York, Canada, Texas, Illinois, Georgia. When I was young and throughout my life, I've traveled to many places. I grew up traveling, and I wanted my kids to experience the same.

We took the Amtrak to Buffalo, New York, and our destination was Ontario, Canada. We had never been there before. I was a little nervous since it was outside of the USA. I love traveling with my kids and exploring. Mariana always loved the adventures with brothers and mom. This trip on the Amtrak took four days on the road, but we got to see different places we had never been before. Our favorite part was seeing the different climates as we were passing through different states.

We had a sleeper cart, so we were quite comfortable, and all the meals were included during our trip. We stopped in different places for a few hours. One stop was Chicago. We got a limo cab and went to a gigantic mall called the *Navy Pier*. We got on the huge outdoor Ferris wheel, which is all enclosed, but it was still very windy and cold. Mariana does not like heights. We had a few hours to kill before our next train ride, so we hung out at this very fancy McDonald's.

Our next train ride was going to be to Buffalo, New York. Mariana always kept up with us and with the boys. I had a stroller for her in case she got tired. Traveling with three kids needs a lot of organization. We had a couple of big suitcases and handbags and lots of souvenirs. When we got to Buffalo, New York, the temperature was below zero and it was in March. We had to wait at the train station, which was pretty isolated, but we were making the best of it. We played in the snow and made a snowman.

I always wanted to teach my kids that even while waiting, we could still have fun. Once we got to Buffalo, New York, it was only a one-hour train ride to the border of Canada. Then we had to switch to *The Canadian* train. They were customs that came on board to check everyone's passports. That took one more hour. Once they checked all our passports, we continued to our destination. When we arrived at the train station,

Our Adventures in Traveling

we had to take a cab to the hotel which was only ten minutes away, but it was very expensive! When we got to the hotel overlooking the Niagara Falls, I loved seeing my kids' faces full of amazement! I was so glad to have arrived at our hotel so I could relax. It was in the beginning of March and the Niagara Falls was frozen. You could see the fall looked like fingers halfway down the bottom of the falls. At night, the lights would shine over the frozen falls and even though it was frozen, it was so majestic to watch during the night.

CHAPTER 15

People Close To Her- Come And Gone

Mariana has shown much compassion towards her peers. A lot of Mariana's friends have known each other since preschool. One thing that Mariana loves doing is helping other kids that need more help than herself.

Unfortunately, Mariana had a couple of her closest friends pass away. That is a very hard thing to experience when one is that young.

One was a boy, and the other was a girl. She met both in preschool. One of her best friends, Jeriann was shorter in stature than her, but pure muscle. They would play together in the playground and were inseparable in preschool. Her teacher took a picture once of Mariana trying to lift her friend up on the monkey bars. My guess was that Mariana thought she was older because she was taller than her friend. Her friend was a year older than Mariana. It was a sad day when we heard her friend passed away a few years ago when Mariana was in high school.

Her other close friend, Mariana loved very much. She was so gentle with him. He couldn't walk or talk. She would lay right next to him during class to comfort him. She would touch his cheek, reassuring him he was going to be ok. She was always wanting to cheer him up and he would smile. That friend passed away in high school as well. I took Mariana to the funeral service. It was difficult to share with her that her friends, who she loved so much and cared for, passed away. I come from a Christian background, and I

People Close To Her- Come And Gone

shared with her they are not suffering anymore, they are with Jesus. This phrase would comfort her and help her deal with her loss a lot better. My words of comfort to her were, "they were no longer suffering," and she would come back to me with the words, "they are with Jesus in Heaven."

One of her other best friends moved away after Mariana graduated from high school. They looked like sisters, and that was hard for Mariana. Her name was Dannie. They became very close in junior high. Mariana was a mother hen to her. The teacher once told me that Mariana would feed her at lunch. Her friend was nonverbal. Mariana had this sensitivity of giving an extra hand or hug when she sensed they needed it.

Mariana loves her brothers very much. Her brothers taught her a lot growing up. Whatever they would do, she mimicked. I remember one time they were playing with cars, and she would start doing the same. They would make the *Shaka* sign, which is what locals sign to say hello. She would do the same. Her youngest brother and her were so close in age that what he would learn, she would learn alongside with him. She was keeping up with him. Mariana was sad when the oldest went to college and a few years later, his youngest brother moved away. But I think the hardest for her was when her dad left.

It was hard for Mariana when her dad left us. At first, I didn't know how to break it to her gently. I told her that her daddy loved her very much, but that daddy was not coming back. When Mariana realized her dad wasn't coming back, she would lock herself in her room. I seriously did not know how she was processing this loss. But one day, I saw her crying in her room uncontrollably. I asked her, "Mariana honey, what is wrong?" She responded angrily, "Dad is not coming back, dad is not coming back. He's gone. He's a bad boy." And then she let out a big, ugly cry for a long time. It broke my heart to see her this way. I knew she was grieving. And at the same time, I was grieving as well. I prayed to God to help me help her.

"God, give me strength because I just don't know how to pick up her broken pieces." All I knew was that I had to be strong for her.

One thing I learned from this is grieving is healthy and we just need to allow ourselves to heal. Some people say that time will heal… But I say God can heal all things and all wounds.

He heals the brokenhearted and binds up their wounds. – Psalm 147:3

CHAPTER 16

Blessings in the Dark Valley

In 2014, I was diagnosed with cancer. This was the scariest moment in my life. My primary fear was,

"Was I going to make it?"

The day I found out from the doctor that I had cancer was the day I felt that my world was crashing down. My mom and one of my sisters are both cancer survivors. I knew I had to stay strong, especially for my daughter. This unpleasant journey seemed long, but I had no choice but to go through it. I had to have both chemo and radiation. The type of cancer I had was cervical cancer. It was stage 2b, which means the cancer stayed in the place of my cervix but was very close to my bladder. They did not want to do surgery because there was a chance of spreading it to my other organs.

The day before I found out I had cancer, I remember dropping off my daughter in school and I had been experiencing excruciating back pain and migraines. I was feeling lethargic all the time. I thought it was because I was working at the restaurant so much. We were running two restaurants and raising three kids; one with special needs. This was taking a toll on me. I was in survival mode, and I needed to hang onto God for my everyday strength.

We had to close the restaurant because we were so much in debt. We were in the mall and the rent kept going up. I would wake up every morning with a knot in my gut. Any ideas I would bring up were laid aside. I felt I had no voice and was not being validated by my partner. That added to my stress.

I remember that day when I got the news that I had cancer. I had flashbacks of when I first got the news when my daughter was born with Down syndrome. Those feelings of fear and numbness wanted to take over. But my survival mode kicked in. I prayed to the Lord,

"You must get me through this. You have gotten me through other hardships. You can also get me through this one."

One thing I learned from this was not to get stuck in fear, but to keep moving towards that breakthrough.

Never, ever, ever give up! Chances are if you feel like giving up, you're right on the edge of your Breakthrough. – Mandy Hale

Perfectly Loved

Special message from her friend

CHAPTER 17

Girls Bible Study

I had started a girls' bible study with a few of Mariana's friends. They would come over once a week. I would have dinner made for them, then we would ask each other, what was their praise report and their highlight of their week. Each one would take their turn to share their biggest highlight. Some would say, I got to go to school and see my friends or I got to be here with you. That would be my highlight of the week, especially during the time I was getting treatment.

I would also teach them creative sign dance. The time I was investing in this group of girls made me forget about my pain when I was going through cancer. It might sound strange, but this was energizing me. I knew it was important for Mariana to have some kind of stability during this season in my life.

I remember my mom telling me one day, "Ana, you need to rest. Why are you still having the girls come on over for Bible study?" I responded, "Mom, because this is my therapy. This is helping me to heal. And I will continue to have these girls come over until I get healed." That was my faith. There's a saying that when you are hurting, it is the best time to give, so I gave up some of my time and this was priceless.

I wasn't just doing this for my daughter, but also for me. This was also the year my daughter was going to graduate from high school. She was eighteen years old, but she could continue to go to school until she turned twenty-two.

I started writing a blog to help me release my fears while at the same time help others who are going through similar situations. I wanted to encourage them. And through that, I was encouraging myself. I believe God has a purpose for everything. Even though these were trying times, I had many divine appointments.

I remember one day I felt a still, small voice telling me,

"Ana, I'm expanding your audience. I am giving you a voice when you thought you had no voice."

This still small voice gave me hope. It was what I needed to get strength and keep me going. I know there were many people in the community who were watching. Some of them would come up to me and give me words of comfort and encouragement. Others were giving me a helping hand.

I had many people help me during my treatments. I also had a wonderful church family who would come over and help me clean the house. Some would help me file paperwork for the business, others would bring us food. And others would take me to doctor appointments which were occurring throughout the week. I think what also helped me was that I knew I had their support. It was time to be taken care of instead of me taking care of everyone else. I wasn't looking for pity. I had to learn to receive and not feel like I was a burden.

I appreciated the people who helped me in my times of weakness.

Going through this cancer taught me I must learn to rest. I felt guilty about having my 'me' time. I didn't have time for that because I was so used to taking care of everyone else. But I realized that if I didn't learn to take care of myself, I could not take care of my loved ones closest to me.

Mariana is very intuitive. She would come up to me when I was having one of those hard, painful days and would caress my head. And would tell me with comforting words, you are going to be okay mommy, you are okay… I knew she was also saying that to reassure herself that she was also going to be ok, as well.

Mariana would call me when I had to fly to the other island of Oahu, to get internal radiation. I am so thankful for my mom because she would help me with the kids. I had to separate myself from the restaurant and all the problems at home because I needed to concentrate on getting well. That was hard for my kids. My son in college came home for a year and helped me and the business for a period of time. I was so thankful that he wanted to do that for our family.

Another thing that taught me during these hard times was that there was someone else who was suffering more than me. One time, while I was waiting for my chemo appointment, I noticed this girl sitting all alone. She had been crying. My friend and I asked her if it was ok for us to pray for her. She told us of other hardships, but once we prayed for her, she felt a sense of peace and relief. Right after that, I went in for my therapy. There was a reason I was there at the right time, at the right place.

Even though there was a sense of anxiety walking through those doors, I knew there was another opportunity I could encourage someone in the chemo room. There were ten to twelve people in the room getting their chemo at the same time for six hours. One day, I noticed a person I knew from Mariana's school and I was able to pray with her and encourage her. She appreciated my prayer. I felt this was one of my missions on being there; it was to encourage and to give hope.

Mariana is always wanting to help. Some things are taught, and some things are caught by example. One time we saw a man in a wheelchair without legs. He was trying to get around on the street. He was dragging a suitcase in the back of his wheelchair. I went up to him and asked him how he was doing and if he needed anything. He said he was hungry. We had just left my work office, and they were giving our employees some doughnuts. Mariana had grabbed two, not knowing we would encounter this man outside a few minutes later. Mariana pulled out one of the doughnuts and gave him one. I thought that was so sweet. Out of the kindness of her heart, she wanted to give this man something she could share. Mariana doesn't like to share yummy things, especially sweets, but this time was different. I'm teaching my daughter about doing impromptu things of kindness. If we give, we will receive. That's a great key principle in life.

Real Love Begins when nothing is expected in return. – Unknown

CHAPTER 18

Celebrations

Just about everything is a celebration in our family. We celebrate the little steps in life because they are big steps for us. Some of the first celebrations were sitting up, crawling, not getting sick, walking, going potty. Other bigger celebrations were going to school, gymnastics, swimming, singing, dancing, bowling and Creative Sign dance, her prayers and so much more.

There was a scary incident Mariana had when she was four years old. She almost drowned in my friend's pool. I was inside the pool talking to my friend and a few seconds later, I saw her drifting away to the deeper part, just a few steps away. I immediately grabbed her and brought her to the steps of the pool. She was shaken up. And I was shaken up even more. She was terrified of the water for a while. This haunted me. I knew I had to turn that bad experience into a good one. I wanted her to conquer that fear.

A few months later, I took Mariana to the YMCA and signed her up for swimming lessons, along with her younger brother. A few repetitions of her going in the water and learning to hold her breath was an amazing breakthrough. That was a big celebration! We live on an island surrounded by water, and I know it was vital for her to learn to be a good swimmer. Little by little, I felt she left that fear behind and started to love to swim.

In high school, Mariana joined a swim team. I learned that my friend Sharon was coaching Special Olympics Swimming. She also helped some students get better at swimming techniques. Mariana did not have any interest in being a part of the swim team in the beginning, but once she saw some of her friends from school joining, she gave it a go.

My heart felt overjoyed and relieved when I saw her become more confident in swimming. She also enjoyed it so much! I went as a chaperone every year just to experience her joy and growth. I loved to see her interact with her friends. Once she won her first medal, her love for swimming started.

Celebrations

Now, Mariana prefers to swim in the ocean. Her love for the ocean began when the pandemic started. The only thing we could do outside was exercise. We chose to swim in the ocean. It was hot during that time here in Kauai, so it was a perfect time to go to the beach to swim. I work full time with special needs, teaching them to develop social skills, learning skills, and healthy skills. What better way to teach them a healthy skill and that was by taking them to the ocean? Every indoor activity was closed, but the beach wasn't closed just as long as we were in the water, we were good. This was the perfect outlet for developing and improving on her healthy skill. Mariana got so used to going to the beach that she would want me to write it on her calendar as part of her schedule. Remember, I mentioned that she's a creature of habit? Rain or shine, if it's on the calendar, that is what we do. Every other week she'll go swimming with my friend Sharon. And every week, a different day that week, I will take her as well.

Some good things happened during the pandemic. Because the Island was closed, the beaches were empty. We noticed more fish, turtles, and monk seals around. We enjoyed the beach very much! This became our oasis.

Mariana keeps active and is fit. Our exercise every week is walking once a week. She likes to walk the same route each week. We will walk close to a mile. It is cool and relaxing. There's a hotel close by that has a golf course.

It is surrounded by beautiful nature, flowers, and lots of chickens. Yes, there are lots of chickens here in Kauai. They started populating after a couple of hurricanes that hit the island of Kauai. The chicken coops were destroyed. So now they are running around like they own the island. Lol.

There was a time we 'adopted' one during our walk. We named her Matilda. That's the name we gave her. Don't ask me why. I think the name Matilda is perfect when you get old. Please, no offense. We would see her every time we were on our walk, and she would follow Mariana around quite a way. Mariana was happy to see her chicken and would talk to her as if she was her owner. We took a video of her following Mariana. She was white and her claws were long and crooked. Sadly, after six months of walking, Matilda mysteriously disappeared. I don't want to say she passed on, but she seemed very old. A couple months later, we saw another chicken like Matilda, but I could tell it was not her. She didn't seem as friendly as Matilda.

Mariana has a good rhythm. Every week she will put worship music on her iPad, put on her earphones, close her bedroom door and sing her heart out. She loves to worship. Sometimes she'll put on a show for grandma. She will sing and dance for her. She won't dance for me. But she will dance and sing for grandma. My mom celebrates her and is so delighted every time that

Celebrations

Mariana performs for her. Some things are reserved for certain people; kisses, hugs, high-fives, calls, dancing and singing. As for me, I have to gently ask her; well, practically beg her for a hug and kiss from time to time.

Mariana likes to surf small waves. There is this group called KORE. This is an amazing organization that enables people with disabilities to enjoy the beautiful ocean of Kauai through a surfing experience. There's a whole team of professionals who helped start this non-profit fifteen years ago and have grown leaps and bounds with volunteers and people with disabilities. Mariana and her friends will join occasionally with this group. She has learned to stand up on the board and surf the small waves with coaching from the volunteers. She enjoys this activity very much.

> *"Happiness is knowing how to celebrate."*
>
> *– François Lelord*

CHAPTER 19

Our Time Together

S pending time together is very important to me. And there are a couple of things we do together at night before she goes to sleep. And I notice that spending time together is her love language.

Mariana loves to watch *Superbook* stories on my iPad and it's a way to spend some quality time together. Every night after we pray with my mom, Mariana and I will watch an episode of *Superbook*. These are animated Bible series as part of an outreach and originated in Japan. It has impacted youths across the world. It has been translated into many languages, including English. We have watched every episode. There are many series and once we finish them, Mariana likes to start all over again with Season one.

Mariana loves to sing, so we pull out the karaoke songs with the microphone. I have a karaoke microphone that is bluetooth. We connect it to my phone. She picks a couple of songs, and we sing our hearts out. We do this sometimes two nights a week. I love doing this with her because it's a way to connect with her.

I've always taught my kids to be adventurous and courageous. Mariana has gone on many exciting adventures. We took a trip to Maui, and I wanted us to do something they've never done before. We went parasailing! The parasailing experience in Maui was the most exhilarating attraction. For me, it was a life-changing experience while we soared like birds above the Lahaina coastline. I felt so free flying high over the water. We went up 400 feet high side by side. As Mariana and I were getting harnessed, I was getting second thoughts. But immediately my thoughts went to

Our Time Together

listening to the assistant's instructions. I had to listen attentively. When we are scared, it blocks us from hearing clearly so I knew I had to stay calm. Then up we went 100, 200, 400 feet! Gradually, it got quieter and peaceful. I was checking on Mariana to make sure she was ok. I talked to her calmly the whole time we were going up, reassuring her she was going to be ok. I was talking to her about the beauty we were surrounded in. "Wow, look Mariana!" I pointed to some seagulls that were not too far away from us. We were up there for seven minutes, but it could seem like an eternity for someone who was terrified. That wasn't the case with us. Once we came down, it was time for her brothers to go up. They had a choice to get their feet dipped or not. I wanted them to experience that thrilling part of the tour, so I said okay. It seemed they were having fun up there until the moment they saw themselves slowing down to the water. Once their toes touched the ocean, they started reeling them in. That's when they realized it was all part of the adventure.

I used to work for a helicopter company for many years and have gone up many times. I wanted Mariana to experience a helicopter ride. We've gone up a couple times. The best one was the tour in Kauai. This is the best place to take a helicopter ride. She got to experience the thrilling views of the entire island. Some of those places we soared over were Waimea Canyon, Jurassic Falls, Mt. Waialeale, Hanalei Bay and Napali Coast.

Perfectly Loved

We even got to see some whales. As we were taking the tour, the pilot described all the history and the different movies people have filmed here on this beautiful island they call, *The Garden Island*.

Mariana likes to walk, but not climb so much. It depends on who she goes with. This one time we went with one of my friends and her brothers. This mountain is called the Sleeping Giant, which is on the East side of Kauai. From afar you can see the shape of the face and body lying down facing up towards the sky, sleeping. The Sleeping Giant is one of three Nounou Mountain trails. It's about a two-mile hike. Once you get to the top, the view is breathtaking. We got up to the "nose" of the Sleeping Giant.

She's also gone ATV riding a couple of times. One time we went with a company that took us off-road riding. We got to see some wildlife and made a few stops along the way where one of the crew members would explain the different movies that were filmed in those areas. This company we went with was very fun! The scenery was breathtaking. Mariana got to ride with me driving. I thanked God that the roads were not slippery that day. I sure would not want to get stuck anywhere. This was a thrill of a ride, for sure!

Mariana has experienced horseback riding. I particularly remember this one time we went with a couple of her friends and their moms. Mariana loves animals, but I must say she feared horses because she's so small and they are so big! We went with this company that was all the way up in Princeville. It was so peaceful. The staff had a heart for special needs. Normally, they charge extra if they need a one-on-one assistance for the tour. But one of the staff said that she would ride along with her at no extra charge. The Ranch Trail ride had beautiful landscapes and was at a slow pace. It included a picnic lunch and a swim at a small waterfall. The horses were very gentle to ride, and Mariana got the hang of it. We will probably go again on a special occasion.

There was one time we went with a few of her friends and their moms on a three-hour mountain tubing journey. They take you into a private property, hand you a tube and a headlamp and take you on a mountain tubing adventure. The waters we went through were gentle flowing, but it was cold! I was absorbing the fascinating views. These waters flow from one of the highest mounts called Wai'ale'ale, which is known as one of the wettest spots on earth. The staff gave us some instructions and historic information about the ditches and handmade tunnels by some plantation workers. Mariana fears the dark and felt a bit uncomfortable every time we would go through a dark tunnel. There were five narrow tunnels we had to go through. If I was claustrophobic, there's no way I would go in one. Overall, this was a fun adventure for the books.

Perfectly Loved

Recently, we went to Disney World this past October for my birthday. I had my sister from Florida stay with my mom to take care of her, while Mariana and I had a long getaway which was much needed. It was a good, long, 16-hour flight. We stopped in Los Angeles for a few hours before getting back on the plane to our destination, Orlando, Florida. Thank God for no turbulence. My daughter does well when traveling. She's been traveling on airplanes since she was born.

I always pray for divine connections when we travel. When we arrived at the airport in Orlando, it was 5:50 in the morning. We took an Uber to our hotel. Because we arrived super early, our room wasn't ready, so we left the luggage with the bellman and took another Uber to get some things for the week at a Walmart nearby. The driver was friendly and spoke Spanish. Mariana associates Spanish with her dad. Though she understands, she just looks a bit confused when people she doesn't know speak to her in Spanish. The jet lag hadn't kicked in yet. Mariana was out of her comfort zone, so at first, she was a bit of a grumbler. How I deal with that is, to stop and listen.

Many people in Florida speak Spanish. Mariana is bilingual. Her first language is Spanish. She will say a few words in Spanish, but she prefers speaking English. My mom will speak in Spanish to her, and I will switch back and forth between English and Spanish. Growing

Our Time Together

up, English was my second language as well. I didn't learn English well until I moved to California at the age of 10 years old.

We arrived back at the hotel to check in, and it looked amazing! The place was peaceful and not too crowded. They had a huge pool. I had gotten a good deal to stay 4 days/3 nights on this property, so we were looking forward to enjoying every amenity.

We got into our swimsuits and went to the pool for a couple of hours. The lifeguard was friendly and started talking to Mariana. So happened that she had a brother who was also special needs. It's neat to have met someone thousands of miles away and have something in common.

Mariana is not used to spending alone time with me on trips. It was a bit of a challenge. We normally meet up with family. But this time was different. Growing up in the restaurant business, I didn't have a lot of alone time with her. I would always bring someone along with us, one of the brothers, her dad, a relative or a friend. This time I wanted to make new memories. I wanted to show her we could have a good time together. It took a few days to get accustomed to that. It felt like being an empty nester in a way. Because she is a creature of habit, she wanted to go home after a couple of days. I reassured her we were going to have fun. A few things on our list were going to Sea World, going to a fair in town, going to a nice restaurant, watching a movie together, going to the pool, going to a timeshare presentation. That last one wasn't so much fun (lol). When I noticed she was getting homesick, we would call one of her friends or grandma. That would appease her for a few days.

Every time we go on trips, she takes her homework and calendar along with a few workbooks that have word search and math problems or writing. I buy her the workbooks that are first or second grade level. It is important to keep her mind learning, otherwise she will forget. It's funny that my mom, her grandma, will have the same workbooks as Mariana. Mariana enjoys teaching my mom.

Our trip together turned out to be another layer of bonding. She is someone that is grown up in her mind and she can be stubborn. I understand the why. If it's not in her regular schedule, she will put up a fight. But once I explain in a very calm voice of the changes and she realizes that I'm not changing the plans, she will end up complying with the new plan. My whole idea is for her to continue to learn new things and experiences. I would say, so far, she's had a good life. What is life if you don't have challenges? Challenges are meant to make you grow.

> *My brother, count it all joy when you fall into various trials, knowing that the testing of your faith produces* **patience**. *– James 1:2,3*

CHAPTER 20

Her quiet spirit – Her Relationship with God

I believe Mariana used to talk to her angel when she was little, in her room. It's interesting that there is a verse in the Bible that says,

> "I surely, I say to you, unless you are converted and become as little children, you will be by no means enter the kingdom of heaven. The kingdom of God belongs to those who are childlike".

The children around us can help us understand that childlike character because they are pure at heart. One of the things I have learned from Mariana is being sensitive to the Holy Spirit. There's been a few times my daughter will go up to an acquaintance and just give them a hug. That person then will begin to cry or get emotional because they needed to feel some loving and comfort.

Perfectly Loved

Mariana gave her life to the Lord at age fourteen. Along with her brothers, they got baptized in the water in the ocean. When she was first born, I dedicated her to God. It's like what the Catholics do when they are babies. They get baptized in water. I wanted Mariana to be protected, and that's why I did that. So fast forward years later, I let her decide on her own if she wanted to follow Christ and that's what led her to get baptized in water. She loves to pray. She will not be shy praying out loud for other people. She's comfortable in her own skin. At church, sometimes they ask if there's anyone who has a praise report. She will get up in front of the church and tell the people in the church her praise report or her prayers. You can understand a few words. If you know her well, you can interpret what she is trying to say. A lot of times I must ask the Holy Spirit to please show me what she's trying to tell me. She gets a bit frustrated when I can't understand her because she knows what she wants to express. I just nod in agreement, hoping that I can understand what she's saying because it seems super important to her. I have learned to be sensitive to her feelings, to listen more, and to slow down for her.

"He who is wise listens." – Anonymous

CHAPTER 21

It's Time to Dream Again

What's next? Something I learned a while ago is this scripture that says,

"Where there is no vision, people perish."

I plan to make a list of 100 dreams- things I want to accomplish with my daughter so she can continue to grow and experience adventures in life. Life can be an adventure, but we need to dream and then plan. I dream, plan, and give it to the Lord. I am praying,

"Show me, Lord, what's next?" And He always does.

After my divorce, I had put my imaginary dreams on the shelf. They were getting dusty, some of them even moldy. Then last year I felt the Lord say to me, *Ana, it's time to heal your heart so you can dream again. And dream with your daughter.*

I got some heart healing counseling in areas I didn't even know I needed. Before that, I felt I was stuck. There were heart wounds and some resentment I needed to heal from. Once I got a couple of heart healing sessions, I noticed my dreaming and goal setting started again. This year I keep hearing, *I want to catapult you to the next level.* When I first heard this, I had no idea that it included writing a book.

I have got many years left in me and so does my daughter. God willing, we will grow old together. I have no time to fear. I left fear back there a long time ago. Fear hinders you; it gets you stuck. It disables you from what God created us to do. Come and dream along and continue to count the blessings God has put in your life and ask the question, *"What's next God? Show me."* And He will. So far, God has showed me that He has Perfectly Loved my daughter. God loves our children even more than you or I can ever love them, and He has hand-picked us to be in their lives.

I want to end with this my friends, with a simple prayer. I don't believe in coincidences why you are currently reading this book. But I believe God has a plan for your life and if you have someone in your life that is special needs, He is always there to help you and carry you. I've experienced it myself over and over. My heart is for you to experience the same and go even further.

Lord, I pray a special blessing for anyone reading this book right now. If they are experiencing any kind of burden or hurt in their heart, I pray you supernaturally heal them. I pray you connect them to the right people so they can step into the greatness you have called them to be. I pray this in Jesus Christ's name, Amen.

If you want to continue to connect with me, you can go on my Website or Facebook Page and check out my next 100 dreams I will be currently working on.

Perfectly Loved

God Bless and Aloha!

> *"I will praise You, for I am fearfully and wonderfully made; Marvelous are Your works, and that my soul knows very well."*
>
> *– Psalms 139:14*

About The Author

This resourceful mother of three has lived in a place some would call Paradise for over 35 years. She has two sons and a daughter. Her daughter Mariana was born with Down Syndrome.

I would describe Ana as being courageous.

There have been many struggles in her life but one worth sharing about is the trials and breakthroughs in her daughter's life. There was a time in her life she thought she was not capable of raising a daughter with

Perfectly Loved

special needs, but as months and years went on by, she realized that she was stronger than she thought. She realized that there was a hidden purpose that was unfolding right before her eyes as she continued to learn new things about her daughter's world.

Ana had been a restaurant co-owner for 20 years and once that chapter closed, she started working as a habilitation assistant for special needs. She's very involved in the special needs community. One of her skills is looking for new ways to include the special needs community, through creating an atmosphere with fun activities and unique events. She loves creative writing, doing crafts, doing outdoor activities, travelling and trying new things in life.

She has led and assisted camps, clubs, Bible Studies, Creative Sign Dance and Proms that have been tailored to include the special needs community. Her goal is to teach her daughter and her community to live life to the fullest and with courage.

A life lesson she's taught Mariana well, is that she's perfectly loved.

Reflections, Dreams and Prayers

Perfectly Loved

Reflections, Dreams and Prayers

Perfectly Loved

Reflections, Dreams and Prayers

www.ingramcontent.com/pod-product-compliance
Lightning Source LLC
Chambersburg PA
CBHW041317110526
44591CB00021B/2822